W. E. Gladstone

Speech on Moving for Leave to Bring in a Bill Relating to

University Education in Ireland

W. E. Gladstone

Speech on Moving for Leave to Bring in a Bill Relating to University Education in Ireland

ISBN/EAN: 9783337324568

Printed in Europe, USA, Canada, Australia, Japan

Cover: Foto ©Suzi / pixelio.de

More available books at **www.hansebooks.com**

SPEECH

ON MOVING FOR LEAVE TO BRING IN A BILL
RELATING TO

UNIVERSITY EDUCATION

IN

IRELAND.

By THE RIGHT HON. W. E. GLADSTONE, M.P.

FIRST LORD OF THE TREASURY.

LONDON:
JOHN MURRAY, ALBEMARLE STREET.
1873.

LONDON:
PRINTED BY WILLIAM CLOWES AND SONS, STAMFORD STREET,
AND CHARING CROSS.

IRISH UNIVERSITY EDUCATION.

Mr. GLADSTONE moved, pursuant to notice, that the orders of the day should be postponed until after the notice of motion relating to this subject.

The motion having been agreed to,

Mr. GLADSTONE then moved that the paragraph in the Queen's Speech having reference to Irish University Education be read. This having been done by the Clerk at the table, the House, on the motion of the right hon. gentleman, resolved itself into Committee on the question, Mr. Bonham-Carter in the chair.

Mr. GLADSTONE then rose, amid cheers, and said : Mr. Bonham-Carter,—I rise, Sir, for the third time since the formation of the present Government, to submit to the House in detail proposals respecting Irish affairs, in regard to which I say little in stating that they are vital to the honour and existence of the Government; but of which I may say also that which is of greater importance—that they are vital to the prosperity and welfare of Ireland. For even if we think that University education is a matter less directly connected with the peace and happiness of the country than others on which we have formerly been called upon more than once to proceed, it must be borne in mind that when we look into the far future the wellbeing of Ireland must in a great degree depend on the moral and intellectual culture of her people; and that in the promotion of that culture the efficiency of her Universities

B 2

cannot fail to be a most powerful and effectual instrument. There are, indeed, those who think, and those who say, that Ireland is a barren field on which to spend the efforts of Parliament, and that the more we endeavour to improve its condition the less return is made for our philanthropic labours. In that discouraging opinion the Government, however, do not concur. (*Cheers.*) The state of Ireland at the present moment does not deter us from asking Parliament steadily to prosecute that course on which it has long ago entered. I will not, when I have so much of necessary exposition before me, trouble the House with details on a subject that is only germane to the matter immediately in hand and that does not strictly belong to its essence ; but I may say, with respect to the condition of Ireland, that industry is flourishing, and that according to all appearances—all well-known and ordinary appearances —the best description of wealth in that country, the wealth of the community at large, rapidly increases ; that order is respected, that ordinary crime is less than in England ; that agrarian crime has greatly diminished ; and, as it has often been observed, and observed with truth, that when agrarian crime diminishes in Ireland, for the most part political and treasonable crime increases, I may state with thankful satisfaction that in 1871 treasonable offences in Ireland had sunk to the low number of seven only, and that in 1872 there was not one treasonable offence. (*Hear, hear.*)

The present condition of Ireland encouraging.

I must again, as on former occasions, ask for the indulgence of the House, for I have to enter on a subject of great difficulty, great intricacy, and great complexity of detail ; and it is only by means of that indulgence that I can hope in any degree to succeed in conveying to the mind of the House a clear conception either of the subject itself or of the intentions and proposals of the Government. There is another plea which, if it were needed, I would offer, but which I know is hardly needed—namely, the plea for that favourable and candid consideration which in 1869 and

1870 we so largely experienced; which enabled us at those
epochs to encounter the difficulties we had then to meet,
and which, I believe, will now again be granted, and will
again enable us to encounter the difficulties with which we
now have to deal.

There is, Sir, a subject of great importance, collateral
to that immediately in hand, to which I will only refer for
the sake of putting it aside; it is that which relates to the
intermediate or proprietary schools in Ireland. It has
lately been represented to me, with a singular and grati-
fying concurrence of opinion, from every quarter representing influence and intelligence in a particular county
in Ireland—I mean the county of Limerick—that the
greatest necessity exists for legislation with regard to the
higher or preparatory schools of that country. I am quite
sensible that is the case; but I am equally convinced that
it is impossible for us advantageously to endeavour to
mix legislation for the intermediate schools of Ireland with
legislation in regard to her Universities. What I wish for
the present to state is, our free admission that legislation
with regard to its higher or preparatory schools, or, at
least, the question how far it may be possible to legislate
with regard to its schools, must arise as a necessary consequence of the legislation which Parliament may think
fit to adopt with respect to the question of University
education. I wish further to point out that the course
which Parliament may take, and the principles which it
may adopt for its own guidance, with respect to University
education will be of the utmost advantage to any Government that may have to frame a measure with regard to
the higher or preparatory schools of Ireland. Admitting,
therefore, the importance, and even the urgency, of the
subject, I trust I shall be favourably understood when
I say that we think it absolutely necessary to keep it apart
from the intricate and difficult question of University
education with which we have at present to deal.

*Intermediate
Education in Ire-
land.*

*Although hav-
ing claims on the
attention of Par-
liament,*

*Must not be
mixed up with
the question of
University Edu-
cation.*

In approaching, Sir, the consideration of this question, it is impossible altogether to put out of view the flow of criticism with respect to the subject itself, and with respect to the intentions and conduct of the Government, which have for some time been almost incessantly brought under the public eye. We have heard much, Sir, of Ultra-montane influence (*hear, hear*), and it may be well, there-fore—that cheer is an additional reason why I should notice the point—to refer to it for a moment. I cannot wonder that apprehensions with respect to Ultramontane influence should enter into the minds of the British public whenever legislation affecting the position of the Roman Catholics in Ireland is projected; and we cannot, I think, be surprised that the influences which appear so forcibly to prevail within the Roman communion should be regarded by a very great portion of the people of this country with aversion, and by some portion of them even with unnecessary dread. It appears to us, however, that we have one course, and one course only to take, one decision, and one only to arrive at, with respect to our Roman Catholic fellow-subjects. Do we intend, or do we not intend, to extend to them the full benefit of civil equality on a footing exactly the same as that on which it is granted to members of other religious persuasions? (*Hear, hear.*) If we do not, the conclusion is a most grave one; but if the House be of opinion, as the Government are of opinion, that it is neither generous nor politic, whatever we may think of this ecclesiastical influ-ence within the Roman Church, to draw distinctions in matters purely civil adverse to our Roman Catholic fellow-country-men—if we hold that opinion, let us hold it frankly and boldly; and, having determined to grant measures of equality as far as it may be in our power to do so, do not let us attempt to stint our action in that sense when we come to the execution of that which we have announced to be our design. (*Hear, hear.*)

But there really, as I shall explain, is no room for any

Fear of Ultra-montane influ-ence.

Should not de-ter us from doing justice to our Roman Catholic fellow-subjects.

suspicion of either Ultramontane or any other influence with respect to the measure which I am now about to submit to the House. The truth is that circumstances entirely independent of our own will have precluded us from holding communications with any of the large bodies which may be said, as bodies, to be interested in Irish University education. The Governing Body of Trinity College, Dublin, have thought fit, in the exercise of their discretion—a discretion which they had a perfect right to exercise—to adopt a policy and to propose a plan of their own, or, at least, to associate themselves with the plan which was proposed in this House by the hon. member for Brighton, with the direct concurrence and sanction of one, perhaps of both, of the members of the Dublin University. That being so, it is obvious that it would not have been consistent with the respect which we owe to that learned body that we should have attempted to induce it by private persuasion to accept a plan of a different character, or that we should have entered into communications with it as to the nature of the proposal which we are about to lay before the House. Under these circumstances the principles of equal dealing prevented us from similar proceedings in any other quarter. Therefore, the door was shut in that direction by no act of ours, but by an act altogether independent of ourselves; and consequently it was plain that the best course for us to take was to look as well as we could to the general justice and equity of the course we felt ourselves called upon to pursue, to devise a plan founded upon our own matured convictions, to spare no labour in drawing up the details of that plan, and to forego altogether the advantage—an advantage often considerable—of holding communications beforehand with the various parties who were interested in the matter. Therefore, the measure I am about to submit to the House is a measure solely of the Government. It is a measure of the Government alone; our

The Government prepared their Scheme without holding communication with any of the religious bodies interested in it.

And the Government accordingly accept the entire responsibility.

responsibility for which is undivided, and our hopes of
the acceptance of which are founded entirely upon what
we trust will be found to be its equity and its justice.
The provisions of the Bill have been drawn up without
any disposition to shape them for the purpose of currying
favour or of conciliating any irrational prejudice, or of
enabling the Government to pursue any other course than
that which the most enlightened patriotism and the objects we have in view must dictate to every honourable
mind.   (*Cheers.*)

Alternative plans suggested in various quarters.

I think it will be for the convenience of the Committee
if I endeavour, in the first place, as briefly as possible, to
put aside a variety of alternative plans with regard to
which numerous critics, who apparently know a great
deal more about our own intentions and desires than
we do ourselves (*hear, hear, and a laugh*), have from
time to time assured the public that the Government
have determined to adopt.   Not satisfied with a single
revelation, these well-informed intelligencers, for fear
the interest of their readers in the subject should flag, have
perhaps in the following week informed them that " the
Government had deviated from the plan they announced
last week, and have adopted another plan," the provisions of which they again proceed to announce. (*Cheers
and laughter.*)   Thus a lively interest in the question has
been kept up.   It was once said by an old poet that it was
pleasant to stand on the seashore and to observe the
mariner labouring on the sea, and it is often a source of
amusement to public men engaged in preparing a measure
of public importance to observe the floundering announce-
ments with regard to it which from time to time are
made by those who neither do nor can know anything
about it.   (*Hear, hear, and laughter.*)

Denominational Endowment.

The first of these suggested plans to which I need refer
is that which is founded on denominational endowment.   I
need only say, with regard to this plan, that Her Majesty's

Government were precluded from adopting any scheme which involves denominational endowment by more than one conclusive objection. Denominational endowment, whether applied to a University or to a College in Ireland, would be in opposition to the uniform and explicit declarations which have been made, ever since this question assumed a new position six or seven years ago, by, I believe, every member of the Government, and, as I can safely assert, by myself. But it is not only the fact that denominational endowment is so contrary to our pledges that if it is to be adopted at all it must be by some other Administration than ourselves. Such pledges are of course in themselves conclusive; but there are other reasons which would compel us to refuse consideration to it, even if we were not bound by them. Were we free in the matter; and were the national convictions upon the subject less strong than I believe them to be, I confess I should think that the plan of denominational endowment in the circumstances in which Ireland is placed would be one unwise in principle to adopt. (*Hear, hear.*) I doubt whether it would be favourable to the true interests of academical learning. I likewise doubt whether it would not lead the Government into hopeless confusion by entailing upon it the performance of an impossible task. The immediate result of such a plan would be an interference of the State with the management of institutions now entirely free, and an attempt, for which the State would be quite unfit, to adjust as between different classes the balance of power within them. If we are to give the money of the public to institutions founded by particular religious persuasions for the advancement of their own views by means of academical education, we must take precautions with respect to the use of that money, and it would be a gross folly on the part of Parliament and of the Government were they to undertake to hold the balance between rival powers with the mutual relations of which they have nothing to do. (*Cheers.*)

Supplemental
Charter to Queen's
University.

Next, Sir, there was the plan which was adopted in 1866 by the Government of that day, which included many of my present colleagues. This measure was founded upon the belief that the wants of Ireland with regard to University education might, in a great degree, be met by extending the basis of the Queen's University so far as to admit of extending the examination for degrees within its precincts to students from other colleges, of whatever religious denomination they might be, or of students who belonged to no college at all. But that plan has entirely broken down. In the first place, the reception it met with at the time was not such as to give us any encouragement to proceed with it; and, in the second place, a proposal that may have been equal to the circumstances of 1866 is not equal to those of 1873. The circumstances of Ireland have changed since 1866 with regard to this matter of public instruction, and therefore any idea of proposing a scheme of that nature has not been entertained by Her Majesty's Government for a single instant. (*Hear, hear.*)

A third Irish
University.

Another plan which has suggested itself to many minds is that of establishing a new University in Ireland by the side of the Dublin University and by the side of the Queen's University, which is also an University placed by its charter in the City of Dublin. Certainly such a plan had one recommendation in its favour—namely, that it would present to us the novelty of the existence of three Universities in one city. (*Hear, hear, and a laugh.*) I doubt very much whether, in any period of the history of the world, or, at any rate, whether at this moment anywhere in Europe, such a singular arrangement is to be found as would result from the adoption of such a plan; and I also doubt whether we should act for the advantage of academical education were it to be adopted merely for the purposes of political expediency, that is to say, for the relief of the Government and of Parliament in a moment of difficulty. Under these circumstances this is not a proposal that I could undertake to recommend to the House of Commons for their acceptance. I must further add with reference to this proposition that the three Universities to be established under it would scarcely have a fair start. The present University of Dublin, sustained by enormous property and powerful traditions; the Queen's University, with its means comparatively limited, and its constitution much more narrow; and the third University, hobbling and lagging behind the second as much as the second would behind the first—could scarcely be said to stand upon a footing conformable to justice. That would not be a state of things that would be regarded by any of us with great satisfaction, and would not be a course of proceeding by which we could hope to effect a real settlement of this great question.

A few minutes ago, Sir, we heard read from the table of the House that paragraph of Her Majesty's Speech in which reference was made to University Education in Ireland; it is a paragraph in so far significant that it draws a broad and clear distinction between the two portions of this subject, which distinction we have kept in view all along. The second of them relates to the rights of conscience. And the rights of conscience are, as we think, deeply concerned in this question, because we hold that there has long been a religious grievance in Ireland, arising out of the existing state and law of University education, and that it is our duty, in offering any proposal to Parliament as a settlement of this question, to make provision for the complete removal of all religious grievances. But, at the same time, it would be a great mistake to suppose that the religious grievance constitutes either the whole or the main question before us. It certainly forms an essential part of it as a negative condition, but the positive and substantive part is that which relates to the promotion of academical learning in Ireland. These two matters I shall endeavour to keep separately

The religious grievance constitutes only a part of the question to be solved.

The positive part is the promotion of Academical Education in Ireland.

in view while I address the House on this subject, as they
have all along been kept separately in view by the Government.   I am by no means prepared to state that there is
no likelihood of conflict between these two principles.   It
is perfectly plain that the old academical learning, which
included teaching in all subjects, must be modified ; because
where there is a difference of religious convictions to be
provided for, it is impossible. to retain the perfectness and
completeness which academical learning possessed in the
olden time.   A large number of Her Majesty's subjects are
at this moment debarred from University training because
they send their children to places of education where their
religion is taught by authority, as part of the training
in those institutions.   Now, it may be said that, even
though this may be true, two questions are to be raised—
first, is the allegation true, and, secondly, if it is true, are
the persons who thus withhold their children from University training right or are they wrong ?   Let me observe,
in the first instance, that the question is not whether we
agree with them or no.   Parliament has advisedly determined to give the preference to academical institutions
which are not denominational. (*Hear, hear.*)   This, in the
three kingdoms, is the Imperial policy, and to it, in all
instances, we shall adhere.   But there is more to say.
When it was observed in former times that the great ma-
jority of the people of Ireland were Roman Catholics, it
was answered, "So much the worse for them ; let them
adopt the true religion, and then all difficulties will dis-
appear."   But Parliament came to the conclusion that
it was its duty to recognize the fact and to accept the
consequences.   There are many Presbyterians who desire
to be educated in a College where their own religion is
taught; and the existence at this moment of Magee
College, under a most able Principal who I believe enjoys
very high repute in the Presbyterian body, notwithstanding
all its difficulties by reason of exclusion from University

Roman Catho-
lics not peculiar
in   preferring
denominational
Education.

training, affords a proof that this belief, that education should be given in connexion with denominational teaching, is not confined to the Roman Catholic communion. I have said it is not our business to inquire whether the Roman Catholics are right in their opinion or whether they are wrong. The question for us is rather this—supposing they are wrong, is it right in us, or is it wise, that they should be excluded from University training? For that is the course which, up to this moment, has been pursued. I do not think that Englishmen, who are accustomed to send their own sons for the most part to those institutions where they are trained in their religion by the same authority that communicates to them the other parts of education, can very severely condemn this error of the Roman Catholics of Ireland, and of some of the Presbyterians of Ireland, if error it is proved to be.

Now, I will look at the question in a very simple form. What is the state of the case as to the actual enjoyment of University training by the Roman Catholics of Ireland? I shall not enter into those details of controversy which have been handled with great ability by gentlemen on one side and the other. There are those who think, and who are bold enough to maintain, that upon the whole, considering who Roman Catholics are, considering how little property they possess, how little it is possible for them to enter upon the higher culture, their state, so far as University education is concerned, is not very bad at this moment. I hold, on the contrary, that it is miserably bad. (*Hear.*) I go farther; and I would almost say, it is scandalously bad. (*Hear.*) I will go into figures, which will at least bring to a test the proposition that I have laid down; but, in applying those figures, I will first protest against the manner in which the subject has hitherto been handled, and will call the attention of the Committee to a distinction which it appears to me they ought to bear in mind in order that they may estimate correctly the facts. In

The case of the Roman Catholics stated.

the Queen's Colleges, Ireland, the total number of matriculated students is returned to me as 708. The number
of Roman Catholics among them is 181, or somewhat

Difference be-
tween profes-
sional degrees and
degrees in Arts. over one-fourth. But my proposition is this:—In the
return there is a fundamental fallacy: the great bulk
of these matriculated students, or, at least, a very large
portion of them, are simply professional students, and are
not students in Arts. But when we speak of University
education as an instrument of the higher culture, we mean
University education in Arts. (*Hear, hear.*) Schools of
law, schools of medicine, schools of engineering, and I
know not how many other schools, are excellent things;
but these are things totally distinct and different from
what we understand by that University training which we
look upon as the most powerful instrument for the formation of the mind. (*Hear, hear.*) Therefore I am obliged to
break down these figures into fragments, and to ask, out of
these 181 students, how many are students in Arts? I now
give the Roman Catholic students in Arts in the Queen's
Colleges of Ireland. From 1859 to 1864, in the three
Queen's Colleges, the Roman Catholic students in Arts
averaged 59; from 1864 to 1869 they averaged 50; from
1869 to 1871 they averaged 45. I think these figures
justify the statement that the numbers are miserably small
(*hear*); and that, small as they are, they are, moreover,
dwindling away. And, Sir, when I speak of recognizing
only students in Arts, I am not hazarding the opinion of
an individual; I am giving utterance to a judgment which
I know every University man will sustain. It is the opinion
upon which the University of Dublin has uniformly proceeded in its handling of this subject. The number of
Roman Catholics matriculated as students in Arts at
Trinity College seems to be about 100. That may not be
the exact number, but, from the figures kindly supplied
to me, it must be within two or three, one way or the
other. Adding these 100 at Trinity College to 45 at the
Queen's Colleges we have 145 as the whole number of

persons whom 4,000,000 and upwards of Roman Catholics
in Ireland at present succeed in bringing within the
teaching of a University to receive academical training in
the faculty of Arts. Well, I think that is a proportion
miserably small. (*Cheers.*) It is something, but it is
really almost next to nothing. Again, Sir, the total number of students in Arts in Ireland I find to be 1179. So
that the Roman Catholics, with more than two-thirds—I
think nearly three-fourths—of the population, supply only
an eighth part of the students in Arts. I think there are
hardly any in this House who will think fit to say that
that is anything like an adequate proportion—anything
like the numbers which they ought to furnish, even after
making every allowance which ought fairly to be made
for the relative proportions of Roman Catholics in the
different classes of the community. Well, I think, then, I
have shown that there is a great religious grievance
in Ireland. Had I been able to point to a state of
things in which the movement was in the other direction—in which, instead of an almost constant decrease of
Roman Catholic attendance at the Queen's Colleges, there
was a steady, healthy, and progressive increase—the case
would have been greatly different. You might have said,
"It is well to wait and see what happens." But I am
afraid if we wait to see what happens, the only result of
that would be to aggravate a state of things already
sufficiently bad. (*Hear, hear.*)

I now, Sir, quit the topic of the religious grievance.
But quite apart from the religious grievance, there is a
great and strong necessity for academical reform in Ireland. I will test the question first as to the quantity or
supply of academical training in that country; and all
along I will keep broadly and plainly in view the distinction between training in Arts and mere professional
training. Now, in Trinity College there are attending
lectures in Arts 563 young men, about the same number

—I think it is a little more—as attend in Trinity College, Cambridge. In the Queen's Colleges the students in Arts are as follow (I take the year 1871, which is the latest I possess):—At Belfast, 136; at Cork, 50; and at Galway, 35—in all 221. Adding these two figures together we get 784 as the total for Ireland of University students in the proper sense of the word; that is to say, in the sense in which it is understood in Scotland, much more in the sense in which it is understood in England. Seven hundred and eighty-four is the whole number of students who are receiving regular instruction in Arts, for the whole of Ireland, with its five and a half millions of population. But there are a large number of students in the Queen's Colleges who are receiving professional education in law, in medicine, and in engineering. The number of these is at Belfast 201, at Cork 174, and at Galway 80—in all 455. Thus, when we include students preparing for a professional career with the Arts students, we come up to 1239. Finally, there are a large number of persons who belong to Trinity College, Dublin, who have the honour of paying, without any deduction, all the fees of Trinity College, Dublin, but who receive from Trinity College, Dublin, no other benefits—and great benefits they are shown to be, or the price would not be paid for them—than those of examination and a degree. The number of these is 395, so that in this way we get up the number of University students in Ireland to the very poor and scanty figure of 1634, of whom less than one-half are University students in the English or in the Scottish sense of the word. Of students in that sense in Ireland there are but 784, against 4000 whom Scotland, with not much more than half the population, sends to her Universities. (Hear, hear.) I think that is a pretty strong case as regards the absolute supply of University and academic training in Ireland.

But the case is stronger still, when we consider the comparative state of the academical supply. Take the Queen's Colleges, those valuable institutions which we should heartily desire to see in a flourishing condition. From 1859 to 1864 they matriculated on the average 226 persons per annum. This is in Arts and other faculties taken together. From 1864 to 1869 they matriculated 1039 persons, or an average of 208 persons. In each of the years 1870-71 they matriculated 200 persons. Thus, as far as the Queen's Colleges are concerned, even the present narrow supply of academic training is a supply tending downwards, What is the case as regards Trinity College? Having a strong sentiment of veneration and gratitude for that institution, which has done in Ireland a large portion of the good which has been done for her at all—(hear, hear),—I observe with the greatest regret the decline in the number of students there. I now draw no distinction between resident and non-resident students; and I find that during the period of years from 1830 to 1834 the annual matriculations were 433. Then, taking a period of 15 years down to 1849, at the end of which the Queen's Colleges were founded, the matriculations had sunk to 362 per annum; while from 1849 to 1872 they had again sunk to 295.

Thus, Sir, we find, upon examining this matter to the bottom, that notwithstanding the efforts of Parliament, notwithstanding the general increase of education, notwithstanding the opening of the Queen's Colleges with large endowments, the University students of Ireland in the proper sense—that is, the students in Arts—are fewer at this moment than they were 40 years ago, when no Queen's Colleges were in existence. (Hear, hear.) I have shown you that, at this moment, the students in Arts in Ireland, even including men who are merely examined and who do not attend lectures, only number 1179; but I find that in 1832 the students in Arts at Trinity College alone were 1461. (Hear, hear.) Sir, I think I have now sufficiently made good my case as to the supply of academic training in

c

Ireland and the necessity of reform so far as such a necessity can be deduced from the mere paucity of supply.

And here I pause for one moment to rebut the charge
that this state of things, though it would not do for Scotland
or for England, will do for Ireland. It is not true that Ireland is indifferent to culture. Irishmen have their vices as
well as their virtues, like every other people on the face of
the earth; but among their virtues has been an appetite
for culture, abiding and struggling for the opportunity to
act even under all the difficulties and all the disadvantages
of their position. (*Hear, hear.*) Look at the College of
Maynooth. Some people will tell me that at Maynooth
there is no culture at all. Now, I will not enter into that
debate; but it surely must be admitted, even by the most
hostile that, if not culture in the broadest sense, it is at
all events relative culture. Allowing for differences of
religion, the Maynooth student is raised by the training he
receives in that College far above his original level, and is
so raised by a course of culture; and everyone who has the
happiness of knowing the accomplished gentleman who
presides over the College will know that such a man would
not be found at the head of an institution where the spirit
of culture was not encouraged. What is the case at Maynooth? Quoting from a pamphlet by a Roman Catholic
gentleman who enjoys one-half the name of my hon.
friend (Dr. Lyon Playfair), and who possesses, I think, not
less than one-half his ability also—(*laughter*),—I find that
during the three years 1866-69 the average number of
entrances was 90 per annum. Since that time, the
income of Maynooth has been cut down to perhaps little
more than a moiety by the arrangements of 1869, though
it receives a considerable income still; but the entrances,
instead of going down, have risen from 90 to an annual
average of 105; and Dr. Lyons distinctly states that, over
and above any advantages that the Maynooth students
derive from the College, it costs each of them on an

Irishmen not
Indifferent to
culture.

average 50*l.* a year to go to Maynooth, the great bulk of these students being, as he says, the sons of the smaller farmers of the country. But the case does not rest upon a casual illustration from Maynooth. It is really an appealing to the whole history of Ireland that she may make a plea for herself, and refuse to be smitten with this condemnation of indifference to culture. Sir, there is a love of letters in Ireland. Ireland is not barbarous in mind. She can say justly on her own behalf—

> " Nec sum adeò informis : nuper me in litore vidi,
> Cum placidum ventis stabat mare."

If only we will give her a tranquil sea in which to mirror herself, it will be in fair usage that she will return to the crew. (*Opposition cheers.*)

Now, I am about to criticize the constitution of Trinity College and of Dublin University; and here I wish to draw a broad distinction. We have been told about forms of government that

> " Whate'er is best administered is best ;"

and I freely and gladly avow, in the case of Trinity College, Dublin, and the Dublin University, that one of the most astounding academic constitutions which it could ever have entered into the head of man to devise has, notwithstanding, through a liberal and enlightened administration, been made to produce great benefits to the country. (*Hear, hear.*) This constitution is in everything almost exactly the opposite of that which, according to admitted rules, it ought to be. The University of Dublin is in absolute servitude to the College of Dublin. But when, twenty years ago, we began to think about the reform of the English Universities, what was the first thing we endeavoured to do? We endeavoured to emancipate the University from the exclusive sway of the Colleges; and that we did in Cambridge, where there were

Anomalous condition of the present constitution of Dublin University.

seventeen Colleges and Halls, and in Oxford, where there
were twenty-four—this .immense diversity producing, of
necessity, a great variety and play of influences.   But
here we have the case of a single University, with a single
College, and the University is in absolute servitude to the
College.   When I say, ."in servitude to the College,"
what does that mean ?   The College is a large and illus-
trious body.   Does it mean in servitude to the whole
assembly of the College ?   Certainly not.   It means eight
gentlemen who elect the other Fellows, who elect also
themselves, and who govern both the University and the
College.   That is the state of things which we find in the
University of Dublin and in Trinity College.   The Provost
and seven Fellows are the persons who appoint, to begin
with, the Chancellor of the University.   He is not elected,
as in Oxford and Cambridge, and, I think, in some or
all of the Scotch Universities; nor is he appointed by the
Crown.   He is appointed by the Provost and seven Fellows.
But, when he is appointed, what can he do?   What is
there the Chancellor of the University of Dublin can do
except by the command or with the assent of the Provost
and seven Fellows ?   As I understand, one of the great
functions of the Chancellor of the University is to con-
voke the Senate of the University; but at Dublin he
cannot do this except upon the requisition of the Provost
and seven Fellows.   And when the Senate is convoked,
the Provost and the seven Fellows, or the Provost alone,
have the power at any moment by absolute veto to stop
any of its proceedings.   Now that is the position of the
University of Dublin in reference to Trinity College.   No
degree, again, can be granted by the University of Dublin
unless it receives a proposal to that effect from the College ; that is, from the Provost and the seven Fellows.
On the other hand, when it has received this permission,
it cannot refuse to grant the degree, unless it votes in the
negative three times over, when the matter stands for

further consideration at the next meeting of the Senate. Well, Sir, these things are singular. They are hardly credible. And now, to crown it all, let me give you the truly Irish consummation. (*A laugh.*) I beg pardon for having used that phrase, but, as I hope to be well-mannered in general towards Ireland, I may be forgiven that single offence. It is, then, a fact that the Senate of the University of Dublin was formally incorporated by letters patent in 1857 ; and it has been acting, as has been always supposed, upon the strength of those letters patent ever since. They have been referred separately to two of the ablest lawyers in Ireland—Sir Abraham Brewster, the ex-Lord Chancellor, and Baron Fitzgerald ; and both of those eminent lawyers entertained the gravest doubts whether—or rather I should say they evidently are of opinion that—the letters patent are invalid, and not worth the paper on which they are written. (*Laughter.*)

This, Sir, is a singular state of things with respect to the constitution of the University, and, certainly, the stranger.it is, the more credit is due to those who have administered its affairs in its relation to the College ; but even this is not all. I have heard the hon. and learned gentleman the junior member for the University of Dublin, in language with which I strongly sympathised, pleading for academic free lom against political party, and against the interference of the State and Crown. But how does Trinity College itself stand with regard to such interference ? Why, Sir, as the University of Dublin is absolutely dependent upon the College, the whole supreme power of legislation for the College lies with the Crown. It can override the Provost and seven Fellows to any extent it pleases. And I will now make a premature revelation for the satisfaction of the hon. and learned gentleman as to what we are going to propose. I hope we shall be able to propose, on behalf of Trinity College, a somewhat more independent constitution than that which it now possesses. (*Hear, hear.*)

Well, Sir, I think I have shown that, if there be anything sound in the principle for which I am contending, and the absolute necessity of which has been, as a general rule, admitted—namely, the principle of setting the University free from the exclusive dominion of the College,— I think I have shown that the present state of the constitution of the University of Dublin calls for interference —although I grant that to some extent you may make for it the same sort of argument that in 1830 and 1831 was made for the old Parliamentary Constitution—namely, that, whatever may be said about it in the abstract, the fruits of it on the whole have been greatly better than could have been expected.

What the University of Dublin is, and what it ought to be.

And now, Sir, while I promise not to deviate from the path which is traced out for me by the subject, I am sorry to be compelled from the necessity of the case to dwell for a while upon the University of Dublin; upon the *question* what it is legally, morally, and historically, and what it ought to be. And, first of all, I desire to clear away a degree of confusion that exists in the minds of some respecting the relative position of the University of Dublin and Trinity College. To this confusion I am afraid our friends in Scotland have made a liberal contribution, because in Scotland the University and the College are for every practical purpose the same thing. According to the old Roman law, as I am informed, *universitas* and *collegium* were as nearly as possible synonymous. I have not lived much in Scotland for nearly 20 years, but when I did live there it was a common thing to hear a Scotchman say to a friend, "Have you sent your son yet to Oxford College?" The University and the College were to him exactly one and the same in idea and in fact. What I want is to sever these words effectually one from

tho other; and I beg the Committee to believe, what I will
distinctly show, that in the case of the University of
Dublin and Trinity College they are in law and in history
entirely distinct and separate bodies. It is not very easy,
perhaps, to supply an analogy to illustrate their actual
connexion; but the nearest one I know belongs to the
beginning of the 17th century. It is in the famous theory
of Hooker, who held that every man in England was a
member of the State, and also a member of the Church;
although it was admitted they were two different forms
of society, yet they presented only two different aspects of
the body politic. In the same way we have had the
University and the College of Dublin co-extensive as to
the persons of whom they are composed. Nevertheless
their academical and legal character has been perfectly
distinct. The University exists apart from the College
now, as it has all along existed, morally and legally
apart, notwithstanding the fact of the identity of the
persons of whom the two are composed. Let me try if I
can prove the proposition I have stated. And, first, I
will point out the separate existence of the University,
because this is the basis of the measure which the Government is going to propose. It is shown, even at the
present day, by the existence of the Senate. The Senate
is not the Senate of the College; it is the great assembly
of the University. Whether the letters patent of 1857
be valid or not is immaterial. The Senate existed before
the letters patent, and would exist without them; but,
besides the Senate, the University of Dublin has other
elements of a constitution perfectly distinct from that of
the College. The Senate has the exclusive right to
grant degrees, although it does so, I must admit, in durance
vile, and under great compulsion; but the College has no
power to grant degrees, they are given exclusively by the
University. The University has a Chancellor and a
Vice-Chancellor, and, lastly, the University has—and this

is very important—Parliamentary representation. That representation is not a representation of the College ; and here is the single case in which the two societies consist of different persons. Many of those who have taken their names off the books of the College continue to vote for members to represent the University in this House, and they are compelled, in order to qualify for that purpose, to retain their names only on the books of the University.

The University of Dublin dates from a much earlier time than the reign of Elizabeth.

The University of Dublin does not, as some may suppose, originally date from the reign of Elizabeth. So far back as the year 1311, at a period when a great intellectual movement occurred in Europe, the Archbishop of Dublin, John Lech, obtained a Bull from Pope Clement V. to found an University (*Universitas scholarum*) in that city. Another Archbishop of Dublin, Archbishop Alexander de Bicknor, obtained a code of statutes for the University. In 1358, Edward III. founded a Lectureship in Theology in the University ; and here we encounter a singularly interesting circumstance, for Edward III. provided in that foundation that, for the purpose of their attending the lectures in theology, safe-conducts should be granted for the resort of students from all parts of Ireland, and that these safe-conducts should be granted not only to the English of the Pale, but also to the Irish enemy, as he was commonly called, from beyond it. It is really touching to see this sign of brotherhood and of the common tie of humanity betraying itself in connexion with the foundation of the University, and in the form of a regulation for securing free access to its benefits. (*Hear.*) In 1364 the Duke of Clarence founded a Preachership and Lectureship in St. Patrick's, which was the site of the old University before the Reformation. In 1465 it appears that the Parliament of Ireland had endeavoured to found a University which, I suspect, very few gentlemen here have heard of, namely, the University of Drogheda ; and the failure of this endeavour led Pope Sixtus IV. to give authority for a like foundation in Dublin, inasmuch as (so says the Pope) there was none at that time in the island, showing that the former foundations had been broken up. In 1496 another Archbishop of Dublin taxed his clergy in Provincial Synod to find stipends for seven years for the lecturers of the University ; and from some evidence of the 16th century it is clear that teaching in some form or other did continue in connexion with St. Patrick's Church until about the reign of Edward VI. It is of singular interest, I think, when we consider the rudeness of the times and the disorganized state of the country, to witness those continual efforts to introduce through an University the elements of humanity and civilization. Across that sanguinary scene of war and turbulence and bloodshed, flits from time to time this graceful vision of an University, appearing to-day, disappearing to-morrow, re-appearing on an after day—

"Par levibus ventis, volucrique simillima somno,"

but, unhappily, never able to root itself on a firm foundation in the soil, like the Universities of England, or like those of Scotland at a corresponding date.

We have now, Sir, reached the reign of Elizabeth ; and here we find that great man Sir Henry Sydney, the Lord Deputy, whose fame has been, I think, unreasonably and unjustly obscured by the more brilliant but not more solid reputation of his son, petitioning the Queen, in 1568, for the revival of the University. In 1585 Sir John Parrott, who had then succeeded to the office of Lord Deputy, proposed to dissolve St. Patrick's Church, for the purpose of founding two Universities, but Archbishop Loftus objected to that proceeding as sacrilegious. Some critical observers put another and less favourable interpretation on the objection —I do not know whether justly or not; but there is some allegation as to the granting of leases of portions of the property to blood relations. However, Archbishop Loftus

afterwards himself proposed the plan which has ultimately
expanded itself into the present University of Dublin. He
obtained a grant of the monastery of All Hallows, near
Dublin, and he prevailed upon Queen Elizabeth to found
a college in Dublin, which college was to be *Mater Universitatis*. It is important to know what was the meaning
of that expression. I will give my own version of it, and
with the more confidence, because something like it has
been given already by one whom I look upon as the
highest of all the authorities who have dealt with the
curious history of the University of Dublin—namely, the
very learned Dr. Todd, so long and honourably connected
with that University. For 150 or 200 years all efforts to
found a University alone had been vain; again and again
it had dissolved into thin air. In the reign of Queen
Elizabeth a completely different policy was adopted, and
instead of beginning with the University, it was determined
to begin with the College. They, therefore, founded a
College, and it was incorporated, but they did not incor-
porate the University, which, as a University, remains to
this day unincorporated. I think that policy was a wise
and sagacious one. The men of that time appear to have
reasoned thus: "Hitherto, the University has pined and
died from want of the proper material to sustain it. We
will supply the material which will feed the sacred flame;
for it is not here as it was in England, where the University grew as it were spontaneously, in obedience to
demand, to supply a thirst for learning. If we plant
firmly a nucleus of teachers and scholars, around it will
gather a body of men, out of which a real and solid
University will hereafter grow." They, therefore, planted
their College and called it *Mater Universitatis*, meaning
thereby that from the College a University was to spring
up, and that other Colleges were to appear from time to
time within its precincts.

Now, Sir, it may appear to some that I am talking

strangely when I speak thus; but I will make good, briefly and I think conclusively, that, according to the original design of the University of Dublin, and as to the continued remembrance—as to the maintenance of that design I will give you evidence for 200 years, from the date of Queen Elizabeth's foundation—there were to be and there ought to be other colleges in the University of Dublin. In 1600, the College having only begun to take students in 1593, the first "commencement," as it is termed, was held, showing that the University was in action as distinct from the College, and this at the close of the first period, when a course of study had been completed by the very first pupils. In 1615, or some say a little earlier, the University Statutes were published, and by them, with modifications, the University has been governed to this day. This was done by the College. It was to be a *Mater Universitatis,* and it was not unfaithful to its trust. Undoubtedly, and it is a large part of the case I have to state, the original design has not been fulfilled; but I do not say it was the fault of the persons connected with the College. It was the fault and misfortune of the times, for not only were efforts made to found new colleges in Dublin in the 17th century, but those efforts took some effect; and I find that no less than four colleges and halls are on record. One was founded as soon as 1604, only eleven years after the commencement of the practical operations of Trinity College —namely, Woodward's Hall. Trinity Hall was founded in 1617, and that, I think, is the one which took some root as a medical College, and subsisted down to about 1689. In 1630 New College was founded, and in the same year St. Stephen's or Kildare Hall. It is shown by these imperfect foundations, made at a time when the mother-College was itself still immaturely established, that those, who followed the founders of 1593, were anxious to give effect to their design of multiplying colleges around Trinity

College, which should share in the enjoyment of the same
privileges; and thereby to bring into existence the true
idea of a University, as it had been understood, and as it
already existed in England, which was the model they
had before their eyes.

But this, Sir, is not all. I will show further that the
most solemn and important public documents have again
and again referred to the intention of founding new colleges in the University. In 1613 James I. gave the University of Dublin the right of being represented by two
members in the Irish Parliament, and in giving it, after
mentioning Trinity College, he speaks of "*aliorum col-
legiorum sive aularum in dictâ Universitate in posterum
erigendarum ac stabiliendarum.*" In his view, therefore,
other colleges were to be founded in Dublin. In 1662 the
Act of Settlement empowered the Lord Lieutenant to erect
another college, to be of the University of Dublin, to be
called King's College, and to be endowed with any amount
of property from the forfeited estates not exceeding the
then very large sum of 2000*l.* a year. The last, and perhaps the most curious, indication I will give is of the date
of 1793. The disabilities which excluded Roman Catholics
from Trinity College and the University of Dublin, were
then removed by law; and an Act was passed which, while
it provided that they might enter Trinity College, but not
share in the endowments of the College, further provided
that Papists might take degrees, fellowships, or professorships in any college to be hereafter founded under that
Act," subject to the double condition that such college
was not to be founded for the education of Papists alone,
excluding all other persons, and that it was to be a member
of the University of Dublin. I think, then, I have shown
with regard to that University that, according to the
spirit and intent of its foundation, it is a scheme which,
noble in itself, remains unfulfilled, and, consequently, presents the strange anomalies in its constitution to which I

have referred. I wish to quote, in a few words, the legal
opinion of Baron Fitzgerald, given, I think, in 1858, Baron Fitz-
with regard to the scope of Dublin University, and to the gerald's opinion as to the legal
question how far it is conformable to its plan that it should scope of Dublin University.
include other colleges with Trinity College. It is not for
me, speaking among many eminent lawyers, to draw a
distinction among members of the Irish Bar, but as far as
I can judge from what I have heard of the opinions and
writings of Baron Fitzgerald on this subject, he certainly
carries in my eye the appearance of a man of very considerable weight, ability, and authority in his profession.
After reasoning upon other matters, he says :—

"The consequences of this would of course be that by the mere
creation of any other college in the University, each and every student
(*studiosus*) admitted to it, whether belonging to that new college or
corporation or not, would become entitled to the University privileges."

I think I have now sufficiently indicated the historical
ground upon which we feel that in dealing with this intricate and most important question it is much better to go to
the root of the matter, to deal with it thoroughly, and to
propound to Parliament a plan which, from its comprehen-
siveness and solidity, might afford promise of giving peace
and of offering finality in that limited but reasonable sense
in which alone it is applicable to human affairs ; and I
propound with some confidence to the House that the University of Dublin, as distinct from Trinity College, is the
ancient, historic, national University of the country, that its
constitution is in a state of the strangest anomalies, that it
calls for reform, and that it is this University within the
precincts of which the reform now projected for Ireland
ought to take effect.

This seems to be the point in the course of my statement Queen's Col-
at which I ought to refer to the Queen's Colleges and the leges and Uni-versity.
Queen's University. We have looked carefully at the
state of the Queen's Colleges, and we have arrived at the

conclusion that the College of Belfast is strongly and solidly founded, and is eminently adapted to meet the wishes and wants of a large portion of the population in the North of Ireland. We also think that the College of Cork, although not perhaps so solidly founded as Belfast, although not at any rate invested with so large a promise of expansion under favourable circumstances, presents what may be called a very fair Parliamentary case, from the number of persons it trains, as well as the efficiency of that training. With regard to Galway College, we have arrived at a different conclusion. I am now speaking, remember, of matter which is not of the essence of the plan of the Government. The essence of the plan lies in what relates to the University of Dublin and to Trinity College; the propositions I now make are collateral to the main portion of the plan, and may be dealt with apart from it, but from a sense of their merits we are disposed to urge them strongly on the House. Galway College, if it has not materially declined, cannot certainly be said to have advanced of late years. The whole number of matriculated students in 1870-1, the return for which is now, I believe, laid on the table, was only 117, of whom half were medical students; and I may observe that, however excellent professional schools may be, they are not institutions which have the largest claims on the taxpayers of this country. (*Hear.*) They are rather in the nature of self-supporting institutions. Education in Arts does not directly lead, as a general rule, to remuneration; but education in Medicine will, I hope, always prove its own reward; and the whole number of students in Arts in Galway, whom I point out as the more proper objects of a public foundation, if public foundation there is to be, is only about 30. However invidious it may be to look to pounds shillings and pence in these matters, and although there come from Galway a certain number of very well-instructed men, even the best article cannot be viewed

Circumstances of Galway College show that it ought to be suppressed.

without some regard to the price, and it is only right I should tell the House that the charge on the Consolidated Fund and other expenses of Galway College amount to 10,000*l*. a year. I have called for an account of the charge to the Exchequer of every pupil in the College, and the return given me is this:—The cost per annum to the public of every pupil is 77*l*.; the cost of every pupil carried on to a degree in Arts is 231*l*., and the cost of every graduate in Law—I confess I grudge this the most, for I know no class which can plead less in the way of necessity for public subvention than our respected friends the lawyers—is 308*l*. The medical charge is lower. We get a doctor, and in almost every case, I am happy to say, a very efficient doctor, for 154*l*. Now, under these circumstances, we doubt and more than doubt whether, when so much better arrangements are about to be made for the people of Ireland, so large a sum of public money ought permanently to continue to be applied to the purposes of Galway College. (*Hear.*) We are disposed, therefore, to recommend, with every proper consideration for vested interests in the Galway College, that measures should be taken for winding-up within a reasonable time its transactions. The measure we propose is that the Council of the Queen's University, which will not certainly be adverse to the College, shall frame a scheme for winding-up its operations at some period before the 1st of January, 1876, a time which will allow every one connected with the College ample time to finish his career.

Vested interests of Galway College to be respected.

I pass on now to the Queen's University. The Queen's University and the Colleges, as a whole, have in my opinion rendered great service to Ireland, and if they have been prevented, as they have been prevented, from doing a great deal more good, it has been by an unhappy if not even a strange combination of influences. I know not whether any one supposes me to be actuated by a senti-

The Queen's University.

ment of either open or latent hostility to the Queen's Colleges; but this I may say that when many objected to
them I spoke and voted as an independent Member of Parliament for their foundation in 1845, and have never
ceased to wish them well. But now I wish to do an act
of justice. It is quite true that the main cause of their
comparative failure has lain in the operation of ecclesiastical influence from the Roman side. This influence, however, has been accepted, appropriated, and made their own
by a very large portion of the members of the Roman
Catholic Church. (*Hear.*) But what I wish to point out,
and it is only fair to point it out, is this. The first blow,
and it was a very serious blow, struck at the Queen's Colleges, was not struck from that quarter. There never was
a plan, I believe, devised in a spirit of more tender regard
for religion than the plan of the Queen's Colleges as it
was framed by Sir R. Peel and Sir J. Graham; and those
who will look back to the provisions of the Act which
established the Colleges in 1845 will see the most distinct
indications of their desire, on the one hand, to keep the
State out of the vortex of polemical differences, and,
on the other hand, to give the utmost possible facilities,
to all who were so disposed, for making direct provision
for instruction in religion within the walls of appropriate
buildings and in immediate connexion with the Colleges
themselves. These provisions most unhappily proved
Who struck the first blow at the Queen's Colleges? abortive; but who was it that struck the first blow?
On the very night when the Bill was introduced by
Sir R. Peel or Sir J. Graham, my much lamented friend
Sir R. Inglis, as member for the University of Oxford, felt
it incumbent on him in the discharge of his duty to rise
in his place and denounce them as " a gigantic scheme
of Godless education " (*hear*). And again, at the end of
the debate on the second reading, so far from softening or
withdrawing the language he had used, he felt it a matter
of honour to repeat it and insist on it. After that declara-

tion so made, it was perhaps not very easy for the representative of Orthodoxy in Rome to accept as sufficiently
religious for Rome what the representative of Orthodoxy
in Oxford had repudiated and condemned as not sufficiently religious for Oxford. I here speak of the Colleges as a whole, and it will be distinctly understood why
with these views we think that the Belfast College and
the Cork College should be maintained; although with
respect to Galway College the case is different, and we
are of opinion that, without the smallest imputation on the
teachers in it, the heavy charge it imposes is not warranted
by the results. I come now to the Queen's University.
We regard its influence as unmixedly good so far as it
goes; but I doubt very much whether, if we succeed in
reorganizing, opening, enlarging, and liberally endowing
the University of Dublin, it would be for the interest of
the Queen's University to maintain a separate existence
by its side. Let me point out these considerations. In
the first place, if, where there are only three colleges,
and where the professors of the colleges form the whole
staff of the University, the University is not very strong,
obviously it has nothing to spare; take away one of the
colleges, and the University will be weaker than it was
before. (*Hear, hear.*) In the next place, we must expect,
as a matter of course, that these colleges will have to
suffer more or less from the competition of an enlarged
and effective University of Dublin, and from the greater
liberty which will now be secured, especially for Roman
Catholics, in choosing the place of their education. In the
third place, if we leave it as it is, it will be excluded from
those liberal endowments which we hope will be possessed
and enjoyed by the University of Dublin. And lastly, it will
have no share in that great advantage, the privilege of
Parliamentary representation, which the University of
Dublin enjoys, and which I hope that University will
always enjoy. (*Hear, hear.*) For these reasons, and not

Reasons why
the Queen's Col-
leges should cease
to be a separate
University.

D

in any penal sense, not believing that the institution is not a beneficial institution, but with a view to the yet greater advantage of those who now profit by its existence, we are of opinion that it will be a wise course if Parliament should be disposed to say that the Queen's University, which was brought into existence merely to answer the purposes of the Colleges, shall pass over into the enlarged and remodelled University of Dublin. (*Hear, hear.*)

And pass into the enlarged University of Dublin.

I come now to the question of the practical principles on which we hope Parliament will conduct that great academic reform to which I have pointed by means of the measure we are about to introduce. By what principles are we to be guided in that reform? Parliament has been recently engaged in reforming the Universities of Oxford and Cambridge; it has laid down very sound principles with respect to these Universities; these principles have not reached their fullest development, but still there they are; they have received deliberate sanction, and it is upon these principles that we propose to go with respect to the University of Dublin and Trinity College. What, then, are the great principles upon which Parliament has acted with respect to the English Universities? First of all it has abolished tests. (*Hear, hear.*) Upon this point there is practically no difference of opinion, because while the whole Liberal politicians of the country have desired that abolition for its own sake, under the circumstances of the time that boon is freely offered with an open hand by the authorities of Trinity College and the University of Dublin itself. But this is a negative rather than a positive reform. (*Hear, hear.*) The next principle has been to open endowments. Where endowments are tied up by particular provisions in such a way as to render them the monopoly of comparatively few, Parliament has endeavoured to widen the access, and to increase the number of those who may compete for them, with the conviction

The practical principles upon which the Government Scheme proceeds are identical with those which recent legislation has applied to Oxford and Cambridge.

that that is the way to render them more fruitful of beneficial results. The next and perhaps most important principle has been to emancipate the University from the Colleges. That is what we did at once in Oxford, and we did it in two ways. The first of them was the establishment of a new governing body. In Cambridge, the *Caput*, supplemented by conventional meetings of the Heads of Houses, in Oxford more formally the Hebdomadal Board, composed almost wholly of the Heads of Colleges,—were in practical possession of the initiative, and were the rulers of the University. We abolished the Hebdomadal Board in Oxford and the *Caput* in Cambridge, and carried over the powers in each case to the Council. And now similarly, that we should establish a new governing body for the University of Dublin is evidently the conclusion to which both principle and policy should bring us. The other great measure of emancipation consisted in the introduction within the Universities of members not belonging to any college at all. Until within the last few years no one could belong to the University of Oxford or of Cambridge without belonging to some College or Hall within it, just as now no one can belong to the University of Dublin without belonging also to Trinity College. Parliament enabled the English Universities to enlarge their borders by taking in members not belonging to any college or hall. Speaking for Oxford, I rejoice to say that Act has been fruitful of good; and already, although the change is a very recent one, there are 120 young men to be found in the University enjoying all the benefits of careful training, but all able to pursue a social scheme of their own, to live as economically as they please, to seek knowledge in the way they like best, provided they conform to the rules of the University; and we may reasonably expect that a very powerful element of University life will in this way ultimately be established. Another method by which we have proceeded, I will not

say to emancipate the Universities, but to make the colleges conducive to the purposes of the University, is a
very important one, and that is, to use a very emphatic
little word, by "taxing" the Colleges for the benefit of
the Universities. That is a principle which has already
received in Oxford a considerable development. We
already oblige Corpus Christi, Magdalen, and All Souls
Colleges to maintain professors out of the College Reve-
nues, not for College but for University purposes; and as
for Christ Church, with which I have been myself connected, though a poor College in comparison with Trinity
College—I greatly doubt whether it is half as wealthy—
yet in Christ Church five professorships of divinity, at a
cost of probably between 7000l. and 8000l. a year, are
maintained out of the property of the College for the
benefit of the University.

*The circum-
stances of Ireland
require some dif-
ference of treat-
ment in detail
from the reform
of the English
Universities.* These, Sir, are the principles of academic reform on
which we have proceeded in England. There are other
principles which it would be necessary to observe in
Ireland, in consequence of her peculiar circumstances;
yet these are the main ones. But there are two points
among those which the special case of Ireland brings
before us, that I must particularly notice. To the one I
would refer with some satisfaction, at least as regards
Trinity College; to the other with pain. It is this. If we
are about to found a University in Ireland in which we
hope to unite together persons of the different religious
persuasions into which the community is divided, we must
be content to see some limitations of academical teaching.
It would not be safe, in our opinion, to enter with one's
eyes open into largely controverted subjects. In theology
no one would wish the University of Dublin, if it be reformed, to teach; and we also think there are some other
subjects with regard to which it will be necessary to observe
limitations that I will presently explain. There is another
matter on which we must pursue a course somewhat dif-

ferent from that taken in England. In England, when we reformed the Universities, we may say we did nothing to increase the influence of the Crown. In Ireland, as far as Trinity College is concerned, I should not propose to increase the influence of the Crown. It appears to me that it may be safely limited. But if we are to have an effective and living Dublin University with a new Governing Body, I am afraid it will be necessary to introduce for a time the action of Parliament and of the Crown in consequence of the unbalanced state of the University at the present moment, a state which must continue at all events for a time. (*Hear, hear.*) When the University arrives at a condition in which the nation can be said to be fairly represented in it, then I think the desire of Parliament will be to carry over to the University itself, as far as may be, the power of electing all its own officers and Governing Body, and to see it thrive upon those principles of academic freedom which have been allowed so much of scope in this country, on the whole with such beneficial results. *Action of Parliament and the Crown necessary until such time as the Irish nation can be said to be fairly represented on the Governing Body of the University.*

Well, Sir, these are the principles on which we propose to proceed. And, now, if the Committee will still have the kindness to follow me, I will endeavour to describe the mode in which those principles will be applied to the University of Dublin. And first, Sir, I must say it is necessary for clearness that the Committee should carefully keep in view three separate periods of time. The first period of time laid down in the Bill is the 1st of January, 1875. It is on the 1st of January, 1875, that we propose that the powers now exercised by the Provost and seven Senior Fellows of Trinity College as towards the University shall be handed over to the new Governing Body, just as in the English Universities the powers of the Hebdomadal Board and less exactly those of the Cambridge Heads were handed over to the new Governing Bodies, which represented mixed and diversified academic forces. The second *Mode in which the foregoing principles are to be applied.*

period, after the 1st of January, 1875, is one of ten years, which we look upon as a provisional period, during which it will be necessary to make some special provisions that I will by-and-by state summarily to the Committee. After the 1st of January, 1885, we think we may reckon that the new scheme will in all likelihood have developed itself so largely and so freely, that the permanent system of government of the University may with safety be brought into play.

I now proceed to explain the leading provisions of the Bill. First of all, the University is to be incorporated by the present Bill, a process which it has never yet undergone. The Universities of this country are incorporated; and it is more convenient and seemly that they should be incorporated than that a particular part—namely, the Senate, as now—should be incorporated in a manner quite contrary to the analogy of our academical history. The *Severance of the* second provision I will name is this—the separation of the *Theological Fa-* theological faculty. We propose to sever the theological *culty both from* *Trinity College* faculty both from Trinity College, and from the University *and from the Uni-* *versity of Dublin.* of Dublin. It appears to us that a measure of that kind follows naturally and of necessity from the changes that have already occurred in Ireland, and from the changes which have been offered on the part of the University and of Trinity College. I own it is not altogether without regret that I personally accede to that measure, for this reason: I think that the University of Dublin has exercised a most beneficial influence over the religious character, tone, and tendencies of a large and important portion of the Irish nation. But still I freely and advisedly believe that we are right in holding that this theological faculty ought now to be severed both from the University and from the College. The details of the operation will be found described in the clauses of the Bill from 10 to 15; and the method we pursue is this:—It is as nearly as possible analogous to the method pursued under the Church Act

in the case of Maynooth College. We hand over the care
of the theological faculty to the Representative Body of
the Disestablished Church. We make provision, I hope
ample provision, for the vested interests of the persons
now holding office in the theological faculty, or discharging
duties in that faculty, as far as those duties are concerned.
We provide that private endowments which have been
created for the purposes of the theological faculty shall
pass over to the Representative Body, that Body to be
subject to the same responsibilities as Trinity College will
lie under, if the Bill be adopted, with reference to the
private endowments in Trinity College. With regard to
the rest of the change affecting the theological faculty,
we propose to follow exactly the analogy of Maynooth.
We ask you to grant 15 years' purchase of the annual
expense; that is, a sum equal to 15 times the annual
expense is to be handed over to the Representative Body,
to be administered in trust for the purposes for which the
theological faculty has existed. And, lastly, as the theological faculty, severed from the University and from the
College, will no longer appear nor have accommodation
in the buildings already existing, we propose that there
should be a charge on the property of the College of
15,000l. to provide buildings for the theological faculty.
So much as to the theological faculty.

I now come to the substantive and positive portion of
our proposal, which I will describe as succinctly as I can.
The principal parts and organs of the University of Dublin
as we propose that they should stand in its detached and
reformed condition, are these:—First of all there is the
Chancellor of the University. The case of the Chancellorship of the University of Dublin is a very peculiar one, in
this respect, that he is scarcely—I speak subject to correc-
tion—more than a nominal officer so far as regards the University. He has indeed the privilege of appointing the

The substantive
and positive por-
tion of the
Scheme.

Present posi-
tion of the Chan-
cellor of the Uni-
versity.

Vice-Chancellor, but then the Vice-Chancellor is, unfortu-
nately, no less nominal than himself; for all that they can
do is, when they are permitted by the College, to preside
in the Senate; and when they preside there they are liable
to be stopped at any moment by the action of the authorities of the College.   But, although he is a nominal officer
as to the University, he is not so as to the College.   In
virtue of his office of Chancellor of the University, he is
Visitor of the College.   As Visitor of the College he has
all the ordinary powers of the Visitor of a college; and
besides those ordinary powers he has another real and important power—namely, that his assent to the statutes of
the College is required, I think, in certain rather important cases, to give them validity.   And so we have had
to consider, in detaching and severing the College functions
from those of the University, what course to pursue as to
the Chancellor.   The course we recommend is this—We
His position think it better, under all the circumstances, to continue
under the pro- the Chancellor of the University as (if I may so speak) an
posed system.
ornamental officer of the University, and, that being so, to
attach the Chancellorship to the person of the Lord Lieutenant for the time being.   This is not a question of
making over an operative State influence.   If it were so,
the case would be materially altered.   But viewing all the
difficulties which beset any other manner of proceeding,
we recommend this as least open to objection.   The Vice-
Chancellor we propose to leave it to the new Governing
Body to elect from among themselves.   He will, therefore, be a real officer, with real functions—namely, those
which attach to the Chair of the Governing Body.   But
we also make provision that the present distinguished
Chancellor of the University, Lord Cairns, shall not, by
the action of the Bill, be divested of those substantive
powers, which he possesses—powers, namely, which accrue
to him in the character of Visitor of Trinity College, and

the whole of which will be carefully preserved. That, Sir, is the proposal with respect to the Chancellor and the Vice-Chancellor.

Now, from what I have said the House will readily understand that an important part of our proposal goes to fulfil that which has remained unfulfilled in the past by introducing new Colleges into the University of Dublin. If the House should adopt the suggestions that we have made with regard to the Queen's University and Queen's Colleges, the two first of such colleges naturally will be those of Belfast and Cork. We shall also propose in Committee on the Bill, if agreeable to the parties, that the two voluntary institutions to which I think I have already referred —namely, the college which is called the Roman Catholic University and the Magee College — should become colleges of the University of Dublin. I will afterwards explain what the effect of that will be. But, Sir, I by no means assume it as certain that these are the only colleges in Ireland which might advantageously be joined to the University. We have not had the opportunity—it was impossible in the privacy which these matters require— of carrying on those communications with the parties able to improve us, which would be necessary in order to enable Parliament or to enable ourselves to form a judgment on the subject. When the Bill is placed in the hands of members—which I have little doubt will be to-morrow morning—it will be seen that the first operative clauses enact that the Colleges enumerated in the Schedule to the Bill shall become Colleges of the University of Dublin. In turning to that Schedule it will be found that it is in blank ; but I have already named four colleges which it is our intention, if the parties are willing, to propose to insert in it when we go into Committee on the measure. And in the time that may elapse—possibly a month—before we go into Committee, we shall probably receive further information to enable us to judge whether it is desirable or not

Introduction of new Colleges into the University.

to lengthen the list. Of course, as I have stated, we do not confine ourselves to the collegiate element, but also allow persons to matriculate in the University without belonging to any college at all.

Constitution of the new Governing Body of the University.

The next change which I have to mention is probably the most important of all; it is the constitution of the new Governing Body of the University of Dublin. I have shown that we strictly follow the analogy of English legislation in substituting a new Governing Body for the old one, and as a necessary step in the process of emancipating—I do not use the word in any invidious sense—or detaching the University. But in the case of Oxford and Cambridge we had, already supplied to our hands, a large, free, well-balanced and composed constituency, to which we could at once intrust the election of the new Governing Body. This, it is evident, is not the case with respect to the University of Dublin. Were the new Governing Body to be elected at once by the Senate of the University of Dublin, it would represent one influence and one influence only. We have, therefore, determined to introduce an intermediate or provisional period, and we shall not ask Parliament to place in the hands of the Crown the nomination of the Council which is to govern the University for that period, but, passing by the Crown, shall ask the Legislature itself in the main to nominate the list of persons for that purpose. I need hardly say that we are not now prepared to bring that list of persons before the House. It would be impossible for us to do it. It was impossible for us to ask gentlemen of eminence in Ireland to allow us to propose their names until we were aware of the general view which they would be disposed to take of the plans of the Government and of the intentions of Parliament; and I have already explained the reasons why it has not been within our power to hold any such communications. There is, however, one point on which I wish not to be misunderstood, and that is the principle on which we shall endeavour to make the selection of names which we shall submit to Parliament. There is indeed another class of members of the Council to whom I shall presently refer, but I speak now of the names we shall submit to Parliament of members whom I propose to call the ordinary members of the Council. They are 28 in number, and will form the principal and therefore the predominating portion of the Council. These names of ordinary members we shall endeavour to submit to Parliament, not as representatives of religious bodies as such, but on wider grounds. For we think that the lists should be composed—without excluding any class or any man on account of his religious profession—from among all those persons in Ireland who, from their special knowledge or position, or from their experience, ability, character, and influence, may be best qualified at once to guard and to promote the work of academic education in Ireland. That is the principle on which we wish to make our choice, so far as we are concerned, and if we make it amiss, it will be in the power of Parliament to correct it.

I will next, Sir, proceed to describe the manner in which the Council is to be brought into action. It will be necessary for it to perform certain preliminary functions before the 1st of January, 1875. It will have to matriculate students, to complete its number as I shall presently explain, and to make appointments of officers, so far as may be needed, to prepare it for entering on its career of full authority. On the 1st of January, 1875, it will take over those powers of ordinary government which have hitherto been exercised by the Provost and seven Senior Fellows of Trinity College. It will have the power to admit new Colleges over and above those named in the Act; it will have a general power of governing the University, and the function of appointing professors and examiners; and it is only in respect to the method of its own election that it will remain under an intermediate or provisional constitu-

tion until it reaches the year 1885, when its constitution
will assume its permanent form.

The composition of the Council will be made complete
from the first. But I have not yet fully described the
mode of its appointment. There will be the twenty-eight
ordinary members to be named in the statute, as I have
already mentioned. During the ten years from 1875 to
1885—the provisional period—there will be—probably
no great number—but still a certain number of vacancies
in the Body which it will be necessary for us to make
provision to fill up. For that limited period we propose
that the vacancies should be filled alternately by the
Crown and by co-optation on the part of the Council
itself. At the expiration of the ten years it will come
to its permanent constitution, and I will describe what
that, as we propose it, is to be; and then the Committee
will be able to judge of the meaning of what I said
when I stated that our desire was that the University of
Dublin should be founded as far as possible on principles
of academic freedom. After ten years, we propose that
service on the Council shall be divided into four terms of
seven years each, four members retiring in each successive
year. There will therefore be four vacancies among the
twenty-eight ordinary members to be filled up every year,
and these four vacancies we propose shall be filled in
rotation—first, by the Crown; secondly, by the Council
itself; thirdly, by the Professors of the University; and
fourthly, by the Senate of the University. There is a separate provision with regard to casual vacancies in the Council,
to which I need not now more particularly refer. The ordinary members will constitute, according to the proposal of
the Government, the main stock or material of the Council
or Governing Body of the University; but we have been
very desirous to see in what way that which we aim at
may meet the general wants and wishes of the people of
Ireland; and, considering how desirable it is to prevent

the action of too strong an unitarian principle—I have, I believe, ample authority for using that word, which is familiar in the present politics of Germany—we have been very anxious to discover in what manner it might be possible to give to those bodies, which I have described as Colleges of the University, a fair opportunity, not of governing the action of the Council by any exertion of influence or combination among themselves, but of being heard in the Council, so that all views and desires with respect to education might be fairly brought into open discussion, and that right might have the best chance of prevailing. It is evident we could not adopt the system under which any one College should be allowed to send to the Council a large number of members. It is also evident that it would not be safe to adopt a system under which Colleges, insignificant in magnitude, should be permitted to claim a representation in the Council. What we wish is this—that considerable Colleges, which represent a large section of the community and of its educating force, should have a fair opportunity of making their voice heard in the Council. With regard to all those dangers which would be likely to arise from too great a rigour of unity in the examinations, or too narrow a choice in their subjects and tone, though we introduce several other provisions on the point into the Bill, it is to the freedom and elasticity of the Council itself, I think, that we should look as the main security against anything either inequitable or unwise. We propose, then, that there shall be in the Council from the outset—that is to say, from the 1st of January, 1875—a certain number of what we call collegiate members, the basis of whose position in the Council will be that any College of the University which has fifty of its matriculated students, those students being *in statu pupillari* matriculated also as members of the University, may send one member to the Council, and if such college have 150 students, then it may send two members. That

Number of members which each College will be entitled to send to the Council.

would be the *maximum;* and this element, so far as we can judge, while it ought to be and will be secondary in point of numbers, would become very valuable and necessary for the purpose to which I have just adverted.

Present Parlia-
mentary consti-
tuency of Dublin
University. The Senate of the University of Dublin, as it now exists, does not, I may observe, discharge one of the living and standing duties which a University is called upon to perform. I mean the election of representatives to be sent to Parliament. The election of representatives for the Dublin University is mainly conducted by gentlemen who, except for that purpose, do not belong to the University at all—that is to say, who have ceased to belong to it, and who are empowered to exercise with regard to it no other Proposed constituency. function. What we propose is that henceforward the Senate shall elect the representatives of the University. The Senate will, of course, consist of all those who are now in it, and of all the doctors and masters who may hereafter have their names kept on it according to the rules which may be in force. I need not add that care will be taken that all those individuals who are now intrusted with the privilege of the franchise will have their rights preserved; but for the future we should lay down the principle that the members for the University ought to be elected by the Senate as they now are by the Senate of Cambridge and the Convocation of Oxford, and by them alone. As to the duty of the Senate, it will be to discharge the duties heretofore discharged by the old Senate of the University, and to share in the election of the Council in the manner I have described after the provisional period has passed, and the permanent constitution comes into play.

I hope it is now understood what our proposal is with Graduates of
Trinity College
and of the
Queen's Univer-
sity will carry all
their present
academic privi-
leges into the new
University. regard to the constitution of the University. And now as to those who are to compose it. I need not say that all the members of Trinity College will remain where they are. With regard to the Queen's University, we

should propose to absorb the whole of its members in the Senate and the body of the University of Dublin, together with all the privileges which now attach to their respective degrees or standing. There is a further provision which we have made in order to accelerate that consummation which we all desire—namely, the rapid introduction into the University of Dublin of those varied elements that we hope will vindicate for it the title of a truly national institution. There is no difficulty in the matter as far as Trinity College and the Queen's Colleges are concerned; because their *alumni* have already undergone University education in a recognised institution. But how are we to deal with Magee College and with any other Roman Catholic Colleges which have not any academic *status* in the eye of the State, and which, therefore, cannot be treated by this Bill as if they had been heretofore possessed of this advantage? In our opinion it would be a great hardship on those Colleges, if their *alumni* were to be absolutely excluded from the Dublin University. We have, however, only a limited power in the matter, and what we propose in their favour is a temporary provision to the effect that during the first three years after January, 1875, the University may, if it shall think fit, introduce into it, subject to examination, persons who have not been at any University, or College of an University, but who shall be certified to have resided for any given time as students of any College which is henceforward to belong to the University, and that an arrangement shall be made to give to such persons the advantage of the Terms which they shall have already kept.

Alumni of other Irish Colleges to be admitted into the Senate of the new University on certain conditions.

I shall now proceed to detail the securities for conscience that will be taken in framing the constitution of the renovated University. The Committee will have gathered from what I have said that this University is to be a teaching as well as an examining University; but it is to teach under conditions in some respects limited. It

Securities for conscience in the new University.

can have no chair in theology ; and we have arrived at
the conclusion that the most safe and prudent course we
can adopt is to preclude the University from the establishment of chairs in two other subjects, which, however important in themselves in an educational point of
view, would be likely to give rise to hopeless contention ;
and were we to propose that the new University should
be at liberty to establish chairs in respect of them, we
should be running the most fatal risk of introducing mis-
giving and mistrust, which might be fatal, with regard to
the rights of conscience in the new University. The two
subjects to which I refer are philosophy and modern
history. (*Laughter and ironical cheers.*) I do not mean
that the study of natural science is to be omitted from
the list of chairs, I only refer to that of moral and meta-
physical philosophy. (*Hear, hear.*) We feel that our
asking for the foundation of chairs in these subjects
would be impossible in the case of a mixed University,
unless we gave up all hope of obtaining for that University the general confidence of the Irish people. And
permit me to say that by excluding theology from the
University we do very little if in that University, under
the circumstances of the present day, we appoint authorised
teachers in certain branches of philosophy, because all
the deepest questions of religious belief are at this moment
contested, partly, indeed, within the theological precinct,
but even more so in the domain of ethics, and especially
of metaphysics. The House may or may not overrule the
Government in this matter ; but, at any rate, that is the
conclusion at which we have arrived with reference to this
question.

There is another important security for the rights of
conscience with respect to the same subjects which I will
mention to the House. We propose that no one shall be
examined for his degree in modern history or philosophy,
as I have defined it, except with his own free will. We

do not think it necessary to exclude these subjects from the examination, provided the submission to examination in them is voluntary. (*Hear, hear.*)

As I have said already, the University is to be a teaching University; but we propose to extend the voluntary principle still further, and to provide that as a rule no attendance upon the lectures of the University Professors shall be compulsorily required from the students. We intend to trust to the excellence of the instruction which will be given, and to the vast advantages the University will enjoy from being placed in the metropolis of Ireland for the attraction of students to it; but we propose to make the attendance upon the lectures of its Professors voluntary.

We propose, also, to exclude the two subjects I have lately named from the examinations for the emoluments of the University. (*Hear, hear.*) From the examinations for honours we do not propose to exclude them, and for this reason. It is perfectly practicable to adopt the system of a positive standard as regards examinations even for honours, and you may bring up to that standard any number of men who show themselves competent to reach it; but as regards emoluments the competition must be between man and man; what one gains the other must lose, and therefore we think it the best and safest method of managing these emoluments to provide that these men should meet upon a common ground upon which all can equally consent to be examined. There are some other provisions of the same kind in the Bill, because I need not say that these securities for conscience are among the most important safeguards of the Bill, and unless they are effective we cannot expect the Bill to work, neither should we desire it to be accepted by the House. Among these, we have provided a clause somewhat analogous to one which appears in the Education Act with reference to the punishment of masters who persistently offend against

E

the conscientious scruples of the children whose education they conduct. We provide that a teacher in the University may be punished or reprimanded if he wilfully offends the conscientious scruples of those whom he instructs in the exercise of his office. But I am bound to say that the main security for the rights of conscience on which we rely is such a representation of all parties, within moderate and safe limits, in the body of the Council, as can be usefully and beneficially introduced into its constitution.

The contribution which Trinity College will have to make to the emoluments of the new University. The next and the last of the more difficult subjects I shall have to lay before you is that which relates to the contribution which Trinity College will have to make to the University of Dublin. It appeared to us in reference to this subject that one principle was absolute, and could not be made the subject of discussion in this House. That was the principle that the present office bearers and teachers in Trinity College should not be made losers by the direct operation of the Act. (*Hear, hear.*) The charge resulting from the adoption of this principle will probably amount on a rough estimate to about one half of the entire value of the property of the College. If this mode of proceeding should be adopted for giving security to their interests we shall propose that the residue of the property of the College shall be divided into two moieties, one of which shall pass to the new University, and the other shall remain the property of the College. The proposition will of course leave untouched the income derived by the College from voluntary payments. This is a principle on which we have already acted to some extent in England; but at present we have not carried it out so far as will, I apprehend, be thought necessary in future. A Commission is at present sitting for the purpose of examining into the property of the Universities and Colleges in England, and there cannot be a doubt, from such knowledge of opinions as I possess, that when that Commission reports, it will be found necessary, after making the most liberal provision for the wants of the Colleges themselves, that considerable sums, especially in Cambridge, where the principle has as yet been applied only to a very limited extent, will be available for the requirements of the University. It is only fair that, as the degrees conferred by the Universities bring people to the Colleges, the latter should contribute to the support of the former. And it will especially be fair to adopt this principle with regard to Trinity College, seeing that it has received all its endowments not simply for performing the duties and functions of a College but also that it might be *mater universitatis*, that its means might be available for an University. The property of Trinity College is estimated in round numbers at 55,000*l.* a year. Between an increase in the amount of the rents and the interest of a large sum of money which it will receive on account of its ecclesiastical advowsons it will immediately have an increment of 700*l.* or 800*l.* a year. The voluntary payments amount to about 23,000*l.* a year, making in all 86,000*l.* a year prospectively, and 78,000*l.* at present. Its expenses are stated at 66,000*l.* a year and some hundreds, and there is a surplus of receipts above expenditure of 11,600*l.* Under these circumstances what we propose to do I will now explain. That mode of proceeding to which I lately referred, namely, the mode of charging the property with the vested interests and providing for a division of the ultimate residue—although it proceeds upon an intelligible principle, yet in practice would be operose, slow, and perhaps vexatious as to details. It would give room for differences of opinion. We have therefore placed a provision for giving effect to that proceeding only in a Schedule to the Bill. In the Bill itself we have introduced provisions of a very simple character, to this effect—that upon the property of Trinity College there shall be laid a charge of 12,000*l.* a year, to be redeemed within 14 years, and at 25 years' purchase. I have already stated that the surplus revenue over its expenditure is more than 11,000*l.*; and 12,000*l.* a year, deducted from 78,000*l.*, which appears to be the total receipt, would leave 66,000*l.*, or, deducted from 55,000*l.* a year, the present estimated property of Trinity College, it would leave 43,000*l.* a year, with an immediate impending increment of 7000*l.* or 8000*l.*, making an endowment from these sources equivalent to about 50,000*l.* a year.*   In truth, after making the charge of contribution which we propose to take for the benefit of the University, Trinity College would remain perhaps the wealthiest College in existence in Christendom.   At any rate I am aware of only one rival—namely, Trinity College, Cambridge, which educates and teaches nearly the same number as are educated and taught in Trinity College, Dublin.   Undoubtedly there are other influences that would act on Trinity College in connexion with this Bill.   It will lose its profits from degrees, which are stated at 2300*l.* per annum.   But there are various provisions in the Bill which would enable Trinity College to economise its operations, and I must say, without fear of offence, that there are great and needful economies to be effected in Trinity College itself.   We have introduced into this Bill a provision intended to facilitate the transfer in certain cases of Trinity College Professors to University Chairs. There may be cases in which Trinity College, as dis-

---

* In this statement is included the value (taken at about 5700*l.*) of the College, Porch, and Buildings, and of the Provost's House. To be minutely correct, this point would require a further examination. The property consists, I apprehend (1) of land having value, but used for ornament or recreation; (2) of buildings yielding actual income in rent; (3) of buildings occupied so as to represent money's worth; (4) of buildings auxiliary to the functions of the College, and thus to the production of the income from voluntary sources. In delivering the statement it escaped my memory to deduct from the future income of the College the sums it will part with on account of the endowments of the teachers in the Theological Faculty. In this case it will, however (for the most part), be relieved of a permanent charge and duty at the moderate price of fifteen years' purchase. It will be charged with a sum of 15,000*l.*, representing, at 4 per cent., 600*l.* a year: but I consider that the borrowing provisions contained in the Bill will confer more than a countervailing pecuniary benefit.—W. E. G.

charging the duties of an University, had to incur the
expense of maintaining a very large and complete staff of
Chairs which may not, and where we think it might be
for the convenience and advantage of all parties that in
some of those instances Trinity College might make over
its Professors to the University, and with its Professors the
charge of maintaining them. These are the leading provisions, which I think contain the essential outline of the
plan, so far as Trinity College is concerned.

I will now point out, in a very few words, what would
be the position of the University according to our proposition with respect to what it will require in order to full
efficiency, and with respect to the sources from which the
money is to be had. We think this University of Dublin,
if it is to be the great national University of Ireland in
accordance with its original design, should be liberally
supplied—first, with the means of teaching ; and, secondly,
with the means of encouraging and rewarding study. We
have not inserted in the Bill any of the provisions which
I am now going to sketch, but it is right that I should
state to the House what our views are, because it may be
thought expedient when we come to the Committee on
the Bill actually to determine the amount of the property
which shall be placed at the disposal of the University
of Dublin. We think there might be ten fellowships, of _Proposed scale
of rewards for_
200l. a year each, given annually by way of reward, and _study._
tenable for five years, which, for fifty fellowships in all,
would entail a charge of 10,000l. We think there
might be 25 annual exhibitions of 50l. each, tenable for
four years, which would entail a total charge, when they
were in full operation, of 5000l. We think there might
be 100 bursaries a year of 25l. each, tenable for four
years, creating an annual charge of 2500l. or in the whole
10,000l. These bursaries would be of the greatest advantage in stimulating the youth of Ireland; and to
establish them would be to do something analogous to

that which has been done with such great advantage by
private benefactors in Scotland for the encouragement
of study in the Scotch Universities. These grants for the
encouragement and reward of study would in the whole
amount to 25,000*l.* a year. The charge for the professors'
chairs might possibly be from 15,000*l.* to 20,000*l.* a year
more, which might create a charge of 45,000*l.* a year. The
other charges would be those for examinations, for the
ordinary government of the University, and for the buildings which would be necessary for lecturing and teaching
purposes. 12,000*l.* a year, as I have said, is the contribution of Trinity College to University purposes from
the fulfilment of which it is to be relieved. 10,000*l.* a
year is the equivalent, or very nearly, of what the Consolidated Fund now pays for Galway College and the
Queen's University. We conceive that a further sum of
5000*l.* a year may be obtained for the University by
means of fees on a very moderate scale. Our view is that
for the remainder of the money required for the purposes
of the University we may most properly and beneficially
resort to the surplus of the ecclesiastical property of
Ireland—(*laughter, and Hear, hear*). It will be re-
membered that this surplus is to be made available for
the national wants of Ireland. The present state of things
with regard to it is this. The property of the Irish Church
was estimated at 16,000,000*l.* The amount charged upon
it from all sources in connection with the liquidation of the
Maynooth Grant, the liquidation of the *Regium Donum*,
and all the rest was taken at 11,000,000*l.*, and the surplus
at 5,000,000*l.* I am told that no more precise estimate
can be given at this date. Parliament has legislatively
declared that that surplus shall be mainly, but it has
not said that it shall be exclusively, devoted to the relief
of corporal wants and necessities. If that devotion to
corporal wants and necessities is not to be exclusive, I
know no more just purpose to which the residue could be

applied than in aiding the funds of the new University.
In our opinion it would be most just to make a call upon
a portion, though it need only a very limited portion, of
the surplus ecclesiastical property of Ireland. (*Hear,
hear.*)

There are only two other points that I have to name
in the very lengthened statement which I am inflicting
upon the House. (*Cheers.*) We do not propose to introduce into this Bill any plan for the internal reform of
Trinity College. So far as we are concerned, we wish
to place in the Governing Body of Trinity the same confidence that they will effect, or suggest, all necessary
reforms as has been placed in the Governing Bodies of
the English Colleges. We propose to relieve it from its
absolute dependence upon the Crown; and to place it
upon the same footing as that on which the Colleges of
Oxford and Cambridge now stand—namely, the footing
on which they are authorised to prepare schemes for the
regulation of their own government, which schemes, when
they have gone through the ordeal of being passed by the
Queen in Council, may have the force of law. As I am
reminded by my right hon. friend (Mr. Cardwell), we have
of course framed clauses for the purpose of at once opening
the offices and emoluments of Trinity College, without any
religious test. I took this matter so much for granted
that I had almost omitted to mention it.

I have thus ventured to sketch the measure we propose
for establishing a free, if I may not say an emancipated,
University of Dublin. Let me say a word or two now as
to the future position of the Colleges in that University.
Trinity College, as I have shown, will undoubtedly no
longer have the exclusive power of granting degrees,
though it must always largely influence by its intrinsic
weight the movements of the University. It will have
a certain diminution of income by the contribution we
shall take from it; and it may, I grant, with respect

*The Bill con-
tains no plan for
the internal re-
form of Trinity
College.*

*Future position
of the Colleges in
the new Univer-
sity.*

especially to its non-resident students, undergo a certain diminution in numbers, and thus the amount of its voluntary payments. But what will it have upon the other side? In the first place, it will have, as I, hope, a termination to controversy—at least to all political controversy. It will remain, as I trust, in its outward dwelling unchanged. There will be nothing to break the course of its traditions. Long—I trust for generations and for ages—it will continue to dispense, more unrestrainedly than ever, the blessings of a liberal culture. It will enjoy self-governing powers, subject only to a reasonable control, and free, I think, from all apprehension of vexatious interference. It will undoubtedly receive some new form of constitution, in which the important and valuable Working Body of Trinity College will exercise far more power than it exercises now, which, indeed, is only moral power, whereas the actual power of the actual Teaching Body of Trinity College, if I understand aright, is none whatever. The present University statutes and the existing system of examination in Trinity College will necessarily form the starting-point for the proceedings of Dublin University, and it will be for the Council of Dublin University to consider how far these may require either expansion or modification. Trinity College will have the means of being heard in the Council, because there will be more, many more than 150 of its members—of the matriculated students of Trinity College—who will be members of Dublin University; and it must therefore have the power of sending two members to the Council. Its students will have access to a large number of additional emoluments. But here arises a question. Is it fair that those who already possess the rich emoluments of Trinity College should have free access to the emoluments of the University of Dublin, such as I have sketched them? The fair rule, as we think, will be this:—In our opinion it would not be right or wise to enact any exclusion of any

person belonging to the University from competition for
the emoluments of the University in respect to his belonging to any particular body, however richly endowed;
but we propose to provide that no holder of public academical emoluments in Ireland—and in the interpretation
clause we have defined what we mean by public academical
emoluments—shall hold any one of the emoluments, encou-
ragements or rewards of the new University, without sur-
rendering the prior academic emoluments which he holds.
The effect will be that a member of Trinity College will
have everything thrown open to him; but he must
not hold both his own and the University emoluments.
He must take his choice, and I suppose he will, which-
ever it may be, take the best. This limitation of plurali-
ties, so to call them, has reference to emoluments of
encouragement and reward, not to teaching offices. For
example, (*A laugh.*) With regard to the Junior Fellows
of Trinity College, there will be no such limitation, for it
would be absurd to apply the rule to a Junior Fellow
receiving only 40*l.* a year—and, I believe, 40*l.* Irish (*a
laugh*) from his Fellowship, and the rest of his income
from his labour. Trinity College will have, upon the
whole, access to a large number of academic emoluments;
and, in common with every other College in Dublin, and
especially with the Roman Catholic University College,
it will enjoy one, as I think, very great advantage to which
I have, not yet referred. The University will place at
its doors, not an absolutely complete, but a nearly complete, staff of professional chairs. These chairs will, I
hope, be held with tolerably liberal remuneration by men
of high reputation, and it will be in the power either of
Trinity College, or of the Roman Catholic College, or of
any College, to consider whether it shall be at the expense
of maintaining chairs, which may in certain cases entail
a corresponding charge, heavy in proportion to their importance; or whether it shall avail itself, without any

F

charge at all beyond a moderate fee, of lectures which
will be delivered at its doors. All these appear to me to'
be important compensating considerations, so far as Trinity
College is concerned.

Position of
Voluntary Col-
leges.

Now, what will be the position of voluntary Colleges?
and I hope they may somewhat multiply, though a Roman
Catholic College is the only one actually existing in
Dublin. They will enjoy an entire freedom as to internal
government. With respect to ecclesiastical and lay power,
I submit that in those voluntary institutions the parties
must settle this question among themselves. (*Hear, hear.*)
If it passes their wisdom to do it, it passes our wisdom too.
All we can do is to give them an open career and fair
play; and I think it will be seen that the access to
University degrees will henceforth be perfectly free
to the members of these Colleges. Together with free
access to University degrees, there will be free access to
University emoluments upon a large scale for them and
for all Ireland. If their numbers entitle them to send
one, or possibly in some rare case, two members to the
Council, they will have the power to make their view,
whatever it may be, known in the Council, and they will,
if in Dublin, have the same power to economize their own
resources to whatever extent they may think fit by making

The Roman
Catholic College
and Trinity Col-
lege not placed
upon a footing of
equality.

use of the chairs of the University. If more than this be
asked—if it be said "this is not establishing the equality
we want to establish between the Roman Catholics and
Trinity College"—my answer is plain. It is that Trinity
College is a public institution. It has been, and it will
remain, under a certain control by the Crown and by
Parliament. But more than that, it is an institution
which (although I admit the operation of this change
must be very slow) has voluntarily renounced its denominational safeguards, and which proposes to make the
whole of its emoluments and offices accessible to all
Irishmen who may be its members, entirely irrespective of

religious distinctions. (*Hear.*) Parliament has adopted
for many years in its policy the principle that these are
the Colleges to which alone public endowments shall be
given. And if I am told, on the other hand, that Trinity
College has a great start in the race, while among Roman
Catholics, and to a certain extent among Presbyterians,
almost everything has still to be organized, I admit the
fact; but I know of no cure save one—to strip Trinity
College bare of its estates and to destroy its whole
machinery. Such a proceeding would really be the creation of solitude in order to call it peace. (*Hear, hear.*)
But it is a remedy which has never been tolerated or even
heard of, and never would be tolerated or (I hope) heard
of, within the walls of the British Parliament. (*Hear, hear.*)

Sir, I feel that the House of Commons must look
forward to the end of this speech with much the same
feeling as it generally looks forward to the end of the
Session—(*laughter*),—and that the sense of relief when it
arrives will be very much the same. I have very few
words more to speak. This is an important—I would
almost say, considering the many classes it concerns and
the many topics it involves, it is almost a solemn subject;
solemn from the issues which depend upon it. We have
approached it with the desire to soothe and not exasperate.
I hope that in the lengthened address I have delivered to
the House I have not said anything that can offend.
(*Hear, hear; from both sides of the House.*) If I have
been so unfortunate, it is entirely contrary to my intention and my honest wish. (*Hear, hear.*) We, Sir,
have done our best. We have not spared labour and appli-
cation in the preparation of this certainly complicated,
and, I venture to hope, also comprehensive, plan. We
have sought to provide a complete remedy for what we
thought, and for what we have long marked and held up
to public attention as a palpable grievance—a grievance
of conscience. But we have not thought that, in removing
that grievance, we were discharging either the whole or

the main part of our duty. It is one thing to clear away
obstructions from the ground; it is another to raise the
fabric. And the fabric which we seek to raise is a
substantive, organized system, under which all the sons of
Ireland, be their professions, be their opinions what they
may, may freely meet in their own ancient, noble, historic
University for the advancement of learning in that
country. The removal of grievance is the negative portion of the project; the substantive and positive part of
it, academic reform. We do not ask the House to embark
upon a scheme which can be described as one of mere
innovation. We ask you now to give to Ireland that
which has been long desired, which has been often attempted, but which has never been attained; and we ask
you to give it to Ireland, in founding yourselves upon
the principles on which you have already acted in the
Universities of England. We commit the plan to the
prudence and the patriotism of this House, which we have
so often experienced, and in which the country places, as
we well know, an entire confidence. I will not lay stress
upon the evils which will flow from its failure, from its
rejection, in prolonging and embittering the controversies
which have for many, for too many years been suffered
to exist. I would rather dwell upon a more pleasing
prospect—upon my hope, even upon my belief, that this
plan in its essential features may meet with the approval
of the House and of the country. At any rate, I am
convinced that if it be your pleasure to adopt it, you
will by its means enable Irishmen to raise their country
to a height in the sphere of human culture such as will
be worthy of the genius of the people, and such as may,
perhaps, emulate those oldest, and possibly best, traditions of her history upon which Ireland still so fondly
dwells. (*The right hon. gentleman resumed his seat amid
loud cheers.*)

London: Printed by WILLIAM CLOWES and SONS, Stamford Street.

www.ingramcontent.com/pod-product-compliance
Lightning Source LLC
Chambersburg PA
CBHW021634270326
41931CB00008B/1026